Ever Unknown, Ever Misunderstood

poems

by

Caitlin M.S. Buxbaum

Red Sweater Press
P.O. Box 870414
Wasilla, AK 99687
caitbuxbaum.com/red-sweater-press

Copyright © 2019 Caitlin M.S. Buxbaum. All rights reserved.

Printing fulfilled by Amazon. No part of this book may be used or reproduced in any manner whatsoever without written permission of the publisher except in the case of brief quotations embodied in critical articles and reviews.

All images are the work of the owner.

ISBN-13: 978-1-7332677-2-4
ISBN-10: 1-7332677-2-7

For everyone I've ever loved

Contents

I
It Happened One Night, All in the Family   1
I Told Her to Use a Thimble   2
Nobody's Perfect, But   3
Mixed Memory   5
Knotty   6
The Conch Shell   7
What Happened Was   8
Hooks, Texas   9

II
The Zebra Sock   13
Billy Collins's "The Lamps Unlit," Misread   14
Ulterior Motives   15
I Heard it On the Radio   16
99% Natural   17
One of the Many   18
Learning Qigong   19
Ever Unknown, Ever Misunderstood   20

III
Coming of Age / Wisdom   25
The body must be a funny thing   26
This Feeble Poem   27
Poem for When I Wake Up   28
For Years and All That's Gone   30
In the Dying Light   31
Reminder: 32
Love Poem, Looking Back   33

Acknowledgments

About the Author

Ever Unknown, Ever Misunderstood

I

It Happened One Night, All in the Family
I Told Her to Use a Thimble
Nobody's Perfect, But
Mixed Memory
Knotty
The Conch Shell
What Happened Was
Hooks, Texas

It Happened One Night, All in the Family

It Happened One Night, All in the Family
that each of us had a dream
that drove us awake — a post-race race,
a journey to the center of a haystack,
and the healing of a girl with pox
in a dorm room, plus the driving out
of demons. Fantastic at best and ominous
at worst, relations of dangers to come
stir us all awake in the world; but
like most films, the stories get muddled
as, with words, they seep into the open air,
and a dream is just a dream: nonsensical fare.

I Told Her to Use a Thimble

A dull *pop* followed by
a soft *ffft* tells me
my mother is sewing,
an unlikely hobby
for one such as her;
I smile and marvel
at the effect of my unborn niece
as I watch my mother's fingers
pluck the thread in and
out of the cross-stitch,
and sometimes, accidentally,
in and out of her own flesh.

Nobody's Perfect, But

Half-way through the joke
about the Catholic priest and
the professional golfer, the
appearance of a rainbow
over the inlet strikes me as
a little bit ironic — watching
God's flood-age covenant stretch out
before our new-age humor
gone dry. Then again, I guess
a colorful reminder of our own
failings is the perfect way of
warning, "nobody's perfect, but"

Mixed Memory

"You decadent little child!"
she says to me
as I dip my marshmallow
into a jar of Nutella before dinner,
and in my head I hear,
"I hope she'll be a
beautiful little fool,"
in Daisy's jaded voice...

Transported into Gatsby's mansion,
my late, sugary snack is now
a tragedy, just part of the scene
concluding Fitzgerald's tale of
failed love, and failed life.

Knotty

Somewhere in the description
of her cousin Andy's
childhood "crash disease" and the
cot with the "crappy chicken-feather pillows"
she had to sleep on at family get-togethers,
my mom shows me a string of memories—
more telling than anyone knows—
without even knowing it. I tell myself,
memory is but a tangled thread
randomly un-knotting itself at
family get-togethers where all the
crappy chicken-feather pillows and
broken limbs somehow settle down
into warm tales told to children
and grandchildren, someday.

The Conch Shell

There are many more where that came from, but none so instrumental to our entertainment; one slice off the nose of that oceanic object and suddenly my sister is out of breath for all the energy she expended trying to "sound the alarm" in sixteenth-century Greece or something and the dog is barking and Mom has her lips pursed too but in disapproval rather than for the task of trumpeting which now falls into the category of Things Not to be Done at the Dinner Table. Well, I took a picture of the event and put it on Facebook, then realized that the extra penicillin pills forgotten on the table will make all our friends think our family has gone completely mad.

What Happened Was

"What happened was," he begins
the story, and everyone knows it's
gonna be good, even though
an excuse doesn't serve as an
explanation in front of a judge.
For now though, we laugh and
settle into our chairs with
enraptured eyes, and the expectation
that things didn't turn out
the way he expected — otherwise,
"what happened was" is as useless
an opening as trying to make it
to the nudist colony in Germany
on an island with muddy shallows
300-yards from shore in a wooden
kayak made by two 14-year-old
boys. But at least
it makes for a good story.

Hooks, Texas

"Well I told you about Hooks, Texas,
population-602-kind-of-schools," he says,
and I have to stop, amused, to muse,
Is this what the English language has
come to, creating five-word-hyphenated-adjectives
or nouns to gag the electronic translators?
But the story continues, my dad going on
about the trials of being the new kid
in a big school—five times the size of
the one in Hooks, Texas—while I smile
to think that this poem could be the thing
to put the "small-town south" back on
the map of fond memories, and curious
expressions on the faces of those who
never knew Hooks, Texas.

II

The Zebra Sock
Billy Collins's "The Lamps Unlit," Misread
Ulterior Motives
I Heard it On the Radio
99% Natural
One of the Many
Learning Qigong
Ever Unknown, Ever Misunderstood

The Zebra Sock

Flung onto the floorboards, I'm shocked
by its presence – I've been driving his car
for how long? and I've never washed
the seat covers? But of course,
that's not what gets me. It's this
sudden exposure to something at once
hilarious and embarrassingly intimate, somehow,
that brings all the memories that I don't have
to the surface.

One errant piece of clothing,
and I'm reduced to a suppressed sadness
belonging only to grandchildren
who lost someone they wish they loved.

Billy Collins's "The Lamps Unlit," Misread

some love it best draped across my shoulders
he said, she said
and suddenly the rumors are off to the races
you know, true though
the words are, voice gives the image a name
and I see the car seat
in a whole new light, the cover creeping up over
the fabricated love-handle,
exposing an upholstered midriff to the world
of passengers

Ulterior Motives

Maybe I have
ulterior motives; is it
like a disease, something
someone can catch, or
observe in my person?
It could be more tangible,
like a treasure chest
or a weapon, I suppose.
But can you blame me
for resolving to
floss a little more frequently
after meeting my
dentist's knock-out son?
Maybe I just have
to eat more ice cream.

I Heard it On the Radio

Let's just say
I live to be a hundred,
and somebody asks me,
"What's the secret
to a long life?" and my answer
is this: "Naps, celebrations, and
anti-oxidants." You might then ask,
"How did you know?"
and without knowing
if the formula worked or not,
I'll say,
"I heard it on the radio."

99% Natural

written on the side of
some fancy facewash
has to make you wonder,
what's in the other "unnatural"
one percent? Is it pickled
pigs foot, or something else
you wouldn't "naturally"
put on your face? Is it
lead-based, or does it contain
something radioactive that
might make you and Godzilla
better understand each other?
Or is it simply
that special ingredient that
makes women slaves to fashion
at some ugly point in their lives?
Then again,
maybe the one percent
is never (naturally)
of consequence.

One of the Many

A working-class man,
a diva, a hipster,
a beach bum, a student (both C and E?) —
each one, one of the many.

Bleached mohawks and lip rings,
suits, ties and skirts,
boots and flip-flops (or any combination) —
each one, one of the many.

A fistful of Starbucks,
a chip on the Armani shoulder,
maybe a rainbow on the sleeve (or under) —
each one, one of the many.

But when I look on such
apostles as these, walking
to their own gospel in chains,
I find that *my* releases
mark me just the same:
one of the many.

Learning Qigong

You can't perfect the *bagua* movement
while you're staring at someone's socks;
nor can you properly perform
swimming dragon if you're watching
that guy's biceps tighten as he stretches
his arm to the back of the room.

If you want to do Qigong,
forget about your broken fingernails
reaching to the heavens,
and that girl's spandexed body
dancing with the *dragon's pearl*.

Instead, close your eyes, and
watch the blur of public life
blend into heightened silence
as the energy moves **you**—
breathe, move, not 'move, breathe'...

Now **shh**, quiet—the *wu ji* ball is forming.

Ever Unknown, Ever Misunderstood

Sitting there in our used and borrowed
clothes, my other and I listen to an old man
tell us how he "let God out of the closet,"
something I never thought
would have been an issue. I chuckle inside
at his choice of words, but still find myself moved
by this essential stranger;
young or old, in love or "in like,"
our problems and their solutions are
bigger than we know, and the source of them
may be ever unknown, ever misunderstood.

III

Coming of Age / Wisdom
The body must be a funny thing
This Feeble Poem
Poem for When I Wake Up
For Years and All That's Gone
In the Dying Light
Reminder:
Love Poem, Looking Back

Coming of Age / Wisdom

Milk-grown teeth turn to cheese
in your mouth, from cigarettes or laughter —
sometimes I can't tell. Maybe your crown
is in your jaw, or perched invisibly
on your head, but either way, wisdom found
a place in your body, with or without
gold. We're the paradox
of reverence and forgiveness in spider life —
plant a seed, bite the hand that feeds, let it bleed, All You Need
Is Love (except when drugs run more efficiently) — but
can you blame us with the headphones
and the computer plugs coming out our ears
and asses? Who knew Satan grew
out of youth in isolation!

...right? You think you've driven over
enough pavement, passed enough gas, handed over
enough passports for a first-class ticket into
senior status, and that a budget-cut menu means
you've done your time
in education, but when did life let go of
learning? Beauty is not the only thing
imagined in the eye of the beholder.

The body must be a funny thing

The body must be a funny thing
for its 'life source' to be so easily
agitated by either an intimate touch
or a hostile customer — or anything else,
for that matter, that manages to mimic
the sensation of falling from an infinite
height — only to realize that the warning
has no bearing on the consequences, and
still the heartbeat returns to normal.

This Feeble Poem

The pen may be mightier than
the sword, but someone
has to be there to wield it;
against the blade of memory
with its glint of imagination,
one might think
that the pen's power
would merely increase exponentially
by osmosis, yet here I am
wounded to the point of distraction
by the images in my head.
What should have been
fuel for the poetic fire
seems to have only turned
my words to ash. Who would have
thought that my sensory overload
could prevent me from being inspired
to write anything of consequence, except
this feeble poem of wanderings.

Poem for When I Wake Up

In the morning, I'll have forgotten
the words you said and the images
I imagined would capture the moment
perfectly. But the one thing
I will remember every morning
after you hold me in your arms
or whisper in my ear
is the poem that could have been,
and the beginnings and ends that form
the poem for when I wake up.

For Years and All That's Gone

A yellow smile in the moon
among the wicked, winking stars
brings me to my knees like
a soft-sounding bird on the sky,
swallowing you whole
in the midst of a love song.
Oh bright bane of hate and
wrongdoing, kiss your heart with
mine and tell the world
we belong; I'll swim in yours
for years, and all that's gone.

In the Dying Light

after Dylan Thomas

Pour my heart out on my sleeve
in the dying light
Kiss your mouth with hungry breath
until I am blind
Sing to dust with Heaven's bells
and love, love me best
in the dying light.

Write me down in deaf black ink
until I am blind
Stir my soul in chilled white wine
and love, love me best
Lick my wounds until they bleed
your sulky secrets
in the dying light.

Light a lamp at Zeus's feet
and love, love me best
Rhyme my heavy head to match
your sulky secrets
Peer around my dusty corners
until I am blind, and kick your bones my way
in the dying light.

Reminder:

thoughts of unrequited love
or misunderstood emotion
dwell in the same place
where things left unsaid—fewer
than those talked of—find
all the more
significance: between sirens
echoing impossibly in my ears
and ocean waves crashing
when there are no fish
to be found.

Love Poem, Looking Back

Whether you write five or five hundred
love poems in your lifetime, you'll know
that each one was a real feeling drawn out of you
(probably with much weeping and gnashing of teeth, on
some metaphorical level) and nailed down on a page
by your traitorous pen, only to glisten
ever-so-slightly—when you pry open your
shame-covered eyes—with the sheen of pure truth
that will always make you smile, looking back.

Acknowledgments

Thanks to my family — in laws and all — for being a constant source of inspiration and support (even when they're not trying to be).

Thank you to all my professors and friends at Gustavus, for shaping me into the thinker I am today — even if they didn't know it.

Other Books by Caitlin M.S. Buxbaum

Songs from the Underground

Uneven Lanes

Wabi-Sabi World: An Artist's Search

www.ingramcontent.com/pod-product-compliance
Lightning Source LLC
Chambersburg PA
CBHW041814040426
42450CB00004B/151